Thinking about the Seasons

Fall

Clare Collinson

SEA-TO-SEA

Mankato Collingwood London

This edition first published in 2011 by
Sea-to-Sea Publications
Distributed by Black Rabbit Books
P.O. Box 3263, Mankato, Minnesota 56002

Printed in China, Dongguan

Library of Congress Cataloging-in-Publication Data

Collinson, Clare.
  Fall / Clare Collinson.
      p. cm. -- (Thinking about the seasons)
  Includes index.
  ISBN 978-1-59771-259-0 (library bound)
  1. Autumn--Juvenile literature. I. Title.
  QB637.7.C65 2011
  508.2--dc22
                          2009052819

9 8 7 6 5 4 3 2

Published by arrangement with the Watts Publishing Group Ltd, London.

Planning and production by Discovery Books Limited

Managing editor: Laura Durman
Editor: Clare Collinson
Picture researcher: Rachel Tisdale
Designer: Ian Winton

Photographs: Chris Fairclough: pp. 28, 29, 31; FLPA: p. 26 (Cyril Ruoso/JH Editorial/Minden Pictures); Getty Images: p. 4 (Christopher Robbins), p. 6 (Rosemary Woods), p. 7 (Vicky Kasala), p. 9 (Stuart McCall), p. 11 (Yellow Dog Productions), p. 17 (Martin Poole), p. 18 (Frederick Morgan), p. 21 (Anatoliy Samara), p. 22 (Louise Moillon), p. 23 (LWA); istockphoto.com: p. 8 (tioloco), p. 14 (Jill Chen), p. 15 (Henk Bentlage), p. 16 (Jowita Stachowiak), p. 19 (Ray Lipscombe),
p. 20 (Gene Krebs), p. 27 (Marcel Pelletier); Shutterstock Images: title page (Maxim Sugar), p. 5 (Petr Vaclavek), pp. 10, 30 (Monkey Business Images), p. 12 (Leah-Anne Thompson), p. 24 (Alexander Shalamov), p. 25 (Marko Vesel).

Cover images: Getty Images: main (Image Source); Shutterstock Images: top corner (Sandra Cunningham), (Chiyacat).

Page 6 *Closer to God, People and a Dog Travelling Down a Forest Path in Autumn* (20th century), Rosemary Woods
Page 18 *The Apple Gatherers* (1880), Frederick Morgan. Page 22 *The Fruit and Vegetable Seller* (17th century), Louise Moillon
"Autumn Leaves" by Aileen Fisher, from *Always Wondering: Some Favourite Poems of Aileen Fisher* (1991), is used by permission of Marian Reiner on behalf of the Boulder Public Library Foundation, Inc. The poem "Harvest Time" by John Foster (1995) from *Seasons Poems* (Oxford University Press) is reproduced by permission of the author. The publishers regret that they have been unable to trace the copyright holder of the poem "Autumn Bird Song" (p. 27). Every attempt has been made to clear copyright. Should there be any inadvertent omission please apply to the Publishers for rectification.

March 2010
RD/6000006414/002

Contents

When I think of fall, I think of falling leaves and cooler days. There is a lot to see and do in fall.

What makes you think of fall?

Fall is one of the four seasons of the year—spring, summer, fall, and winter.

The days get shorter in the fall, and the nights get longer.

Do you know which kind of tree has acorns?

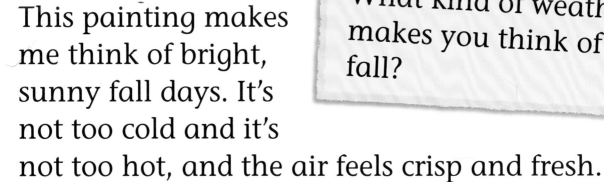

This painting makes me think of bright, sunny fall days. It's not too cold and it's not too hot, and the air feels crisp and fresh.

What kind of weather makes you think of fall?

On some fall days, the weather is dry and the sky is blue. Other days are cloudy, wet, and windy, and the air feels damp and cold.

Have you seen leaves being tossed by blustery fall winds?

In late fall, I sometimes feel cold when I get out of bed. When I go outside, there may be frost on the ground.

Why do you think frost forms when it is very cold at night?

Sometimes in fall it is foggy or misty when I walk to school. When it's foggy, it can be hard to see things that are far away.

As the weather gets colder in fall, I need to wear warmer clothes.

On cool fall days, I wear a sweater, pants, and a jacket. When it's really cold, I wear a hat and gloves, too.

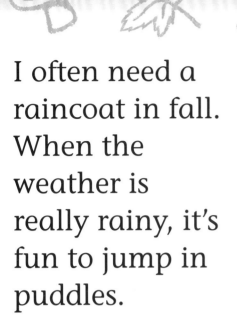

I often need a raincoat in fall. When the weather is really rainy, it's fun to jump in puddles.

What clothes do you wear in fall?

In fall, I love to play in piles of crisp, crunchy leaves. At this time of year, leaves turn from green to yellow, orange, red, and brown. Then they fall to the ground.

Why do you think we call this season fall?

Autumn Leaves

One of the nicest beds I know
isn't a bed of soft white snow,
isn't a bed of cool green grass
after the noisy mowers pass,
isn't a bed of yellow hay
making me itch for all a day—
but autumn leaves in a pile that high,
deep, and smelling like fall, and dry.
That's the bed where I like to lie
and watch the flutters go by.

Aileen Fisher

I love going to the woods in fall. It's fun to search for nuts and pinecones on the ground.

Have you ever found nuts on the ground in fall?

Why should children never pick and eat mushrooms that grow in the wild?

In fall, I sometimes see mushrooms and toadstools growing in the woods, too.

Many plants rest in fall, but there are still lots of jobs to do in the backyard.

Gardeners must protect their plants from frost and make sure their gardens are ready for winter. I like to rake up fallen leaves.

Fall is a good time for pruning and planting. In the vegetable garden, lots of crops are ready to pick.

Which fall vegetables can you see in this picture?

This painting makes me think of juicy, ripe apples. Fall is the season when many kinds of orchard fruits are ready to pick.

Do you know any other kinds of fruit that grow on trees?

In fall, I love to pick wild blackberries from hedges and in woods. Blackberries are really tasty, but the plants have sharp thorns!

How can you tell if a blackberry is ripe?

In fall, I often see farmers plowing their fields. Fall is a busy time for farmers. They harvest their vegetables, prepare the soil, and plant seeds.

Harvest Time

Harvest time! Harvest time!
It's harvest time again.
Time to cut the corn
and gather in the grain.

Harvest time! Harvest time!
Time to pick the fruits,
to gather in the nuts,
and dig up all the roots.

Harvest time! Harvest time!
In the autumn sun
We'll cut, pick, and dig
until the harvest's done.

John Foster

This painting makes me think of delicious fall food. Apples are crunchy and cabbages are tasty at this time of year.

What kinds of fruits and vegetables can you see in this picture?

As the weather gets colder, I like to eat warm food. I especially like the flavor of healthy alphabet vegetable soup.

What is your favorite kind of soup?

When I go to the park in fall, I sometimes see squirrels gathering food. They store up nuts and seeds and eat them during the cold winter months ahead.

Other animals, such as some frogs, find safe places to hide in fall. Then they go into a deep sleep called hibernation. They will wake when the weather gets warmer in spring.

Do you know any other animals that hibernate?

Have you noticed flocks of birds perching on power lines in the fall? When the weather gets colder, some birds migrate.

They gather together and fly south where the weather is warmer and food is easier to find. The birds will return next spring.

Autumn Bird Song

Over the housetops,
Over the trees,
Winging their way
In a stiff fall breeze.

A flock of birds
Is flying along
Southward, for winter,
Singing a song.

Singing a song
They all like to sing,
"We'll see you again
When it's spring, spring, spring."

After the long summer vacation, I look forward to going back to school in fall. It's exciting to start a new school year and see my friends again. It's fun to make new friends, too.

At school in fall, we play lots of games outside. I like to play team games such as soccer and basketball.

What games do you like playing at school in fall?

When I think of fall, I think of Halloween
and Thanksgiving! On Halloween, I like to
put on a costume and go trick-or-treating.
On Thanksgiving, we roast a huge turkey
for dinner.

As the months of fall go by, the days get shorter and colder. It gets dark early and I spend more time inside. When I play outside, I need to dress up really warmly. Soon it will be winter.

How is winter different from fall?

Index